I0002589

Orations Of John Quincy Adams:

Oration At Plymouth; Lafayette;

The Jubilee Of The Constitution

John Quincy Adams

KESSINGER
PUBLISHING

JOHN QUINCY ADAMS

(1767–1848)

No other American President, not even Thomas Jefferson, has equaled John Quincy Adams in literary accomplishments. His orations and public speeches will be found to stand for a tradition of painstaking, scholastic finish hardly to be found elsewhere in American orations, and certainly not among the speeches of any other President. As a result of the pains he took with them, they belong rather to literature than to politics, and it is possible that they will not be generally appreciated at their real worth for several generations still to come. If, as is sometimes alleged in such cases, they gain in literary finish at the expense of force, it is not to be forgotten that the forcible speech which, ignoring all rules, carries its point by assault, may buy immediate effect at the expense of permanent respectability. And if John Quincy Adams, who labored as Cicero did to give his addresses the greatest possible literary finish, does not rank with Cicero among orators, it is certain that respectability will always be willingly conceded him by every generation of his countrymen.

Some idea of the extent of his early studies may be gained from his father's letter to Benjamin Waterhouse, written from Auteuil, France, in 1785. John Quincy Adams being then only in his eighteenth year, the elder Adams said of him:—

«If you were to examine him in English and French poetry, I know not where you would find anybody his superior; in Roman and English history few persons of his age. It is rare to find a youth possessed of such knowledge. He has translated Virgil's ‹Æneid,› ‹Suetonius,› the whole of ‹Sallust›; ‹Tacitus,› ‹Agricola›; his ‹Germany› and several other books of his ‹Annals,› a great part of Horace, some of Ovid, and some of Cæsar's ‹Commentaries,› in writing, besides a number of Tully's orations. . . . In Greek his progress has not been equal, yet he has studied morsels in Aristotle's ‹Poetics,› in Plutarch's ‹Lives,› and Lucian's ‹Dialogues,› ‹The Choice of Hercules,› in Xenophon, and lately he has gone through several books of Homer's ‹Iliad.›»

The elder Adams concludes the list of his son's accomplishments with a catalogue of his labors in mathematics hardly inferior in length to that cited in the classics. Even if it were true, as has been urged by the political opponents of the Adams family, that no one of its members has ever shown more than respectable natural talent,

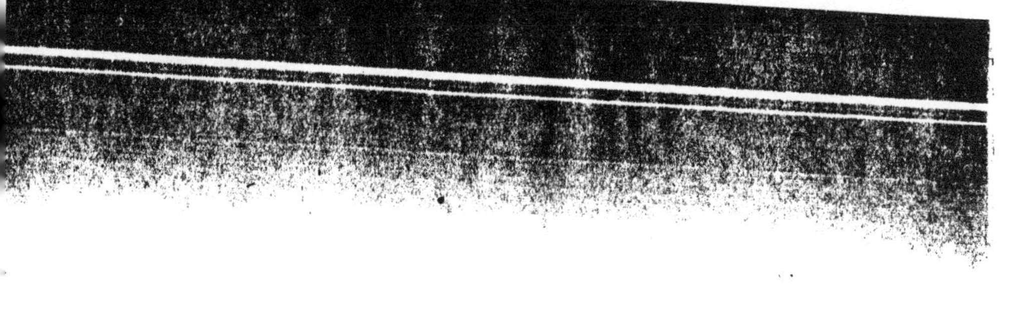

DEPARTURE OF THE PILGRIM FATHERS FROM DELFT HAVEN.

Photogravure after the Original by Charles W. Cope.

THE «Pilgrim Fathers» who landed at Plymouth from the Mayflower, December 25th, 1620, sailed from Southampton, where they had been joined by those who had left Delft Haven, Holland, in the Speedwell some weeks before.

it would add overwhelming weight to the argument in favor of the laborious habits of study which have characterized them to the third and fourth generations, and, from the time of John Adams until our own, have made them men of mark and far-reaching national influence.

In national politics, John Quincy Adams, the last of the line of colonial gentlemen who achieved the presidency, stood for education, for rigid ideas of moral duty, for dignity, for patriotism, for all the virtues which are best cultivated through processes of segregation. He ended an epoch in which it was possible for a man who, as he did, wrote 'Poems on Religion and Society' and paraphrased the Psalms into English verse to be elected President. It has hardly been possible since his day.

Chosen as a Democrat in 1825, Mr. Adams was really the first Whig President. His speeches are important, historically, because they define political tendencies as a result of which the Whig party took the place of the Federalist.

ORATION AT PLYMOUTH

(Delivered at Plymouth on the Twenty-Second Day of December, 1802, in Commemoration of the Landing of the Pilgrims)

Among the sentiments of most powerful operation upon the human heart, and most highly honorable to the human character, are those of veneration for our forefathers, and of love for our posterity. They form the connecting links between the selfish and the social passions. By the fundamental principle of Christianity, the happiness of the individual is interwoven, by innumerable and imperceptible ties, with that of his contemporaries. By the power of filial reverence and parental affection, individual existence is extended beyond the limits of individual life, and the happiness of every age is chained in mutual dependence upon that of every other. Respect for his ancestors excites, in the breast of man, interest in their history, attachment to their characters, concern for their errors, involuntary pride in their virtues. Love for his posterity spurs him to exertion for their support, stimulates him to virtue for their example, and fills him with the tenderest solicitude for their welfare. Man, therefore, was not made for himself alone. No, he was made for his country, by the obligations of the social compact; he was made for his species, by the Christian duties of universal charity; he was made for all ages past, by the sentiment of reverence for his forefathers; and he was made for all future times, by the impulse of affection for his progeny. Under the influence of these principles,

«Existence sees him spurn her bounded reign.»

They redeem his nature from the subjection of time and space; he is no longer a «puny insect shivering at a breeze»; he is the glory of creation, formed to occupy all time and all extent; bounded, during his residence upon earth, only to the boundaries of the world, and destined to life and immortality in brighter regions, when the fabric of nature itself shall dissolve and perish.

The voice of history has not, in all its compass, a note but answers in unison with these sentiments. The barbarian chieftain, who defended his country against the Roman invasion, driven to the remotest extremity of Britain, and stimulating his followers to battle by all that has power of persuasion upon the human heart, concluded his persuasion by an appeal to these irresistible feelings: «Think of your forefathers and of your posterity.» The Romans themselves, at the pinnacle of civilization, were actuated by the same impressions, and celebrated, in anniversary festivals, every great event which had signalized the annals of their forefathers. To multiply instances where it were impossible to adduce an exception would be to waste your time and abuse your patience; but in the sacred volume, which contains the substance of our firmest faith and of our most precious hopes, these passions not only maintain their highest efficacy, but are sanctioned by the express injunctions of the Divine Legislator to his chosen people.

The revolutions of time furnish no previous example of a nation shooting up to maturity and expanding into greatness with the rapidity which has characterized the growth of the American people. In the luxuriance of youth, and in the vigor of manhood, it is pleasing and instructive to look backwards upon the helpless days of infancy; but in the continual and essential changes of a growing subject, the transactions of that early period would be soon obliterated from the memory but for some periodical call of attention to aid the silent records of the historian. Such celebrations arouse and gratify the kindliest emotions of the bosom. They are faithful pledges of the respect we bear to the memory of our ancestors and of the tenderness with which we cherish the rising generation. They introduce the sages and heroes of ages past to the notice and emulation of succeeding times; they are at once testimonials of our gratitude, and schools of virtue to our children.

These sentiments are wise; they are honorable; they are virtuous; their cultivation is not merely innocent pleasure, it is incumbent duty. Obedient to their dictates, you, my fellow-citizens, have instituted and paid frequent observance to this annual solemnity. And what event of weightier intrinsic importance, or of more extensive consequences, was ever selected for this honorary distinction?

In reverting to the period of our origin, other nations have generally been compelled to plunge into the chaos of impenetrable antiquity, or to trace a lawless ancestry into the caverns of ravishers and robbers. It is your peculiar privilege to commemorate, in this birthday of your nation, an event ascertained in its minutest details; an event of which the principal actors are known to you familiarly, as if belonging to your own age; an event of a magnitude before which imagination shrinks at the imperfection of her powers. It is your further happiness to behold, in those eminent characters, who were most conspicuous in accomplishing the settlement of your country, men upon whose virtue you can dwell with honest exultation. The founders of your race are not handed down to you, like the father of the Roman people, as the sucklings of a wolf. You are not descended from a nauseous compound of fanaticism and sensuality, whose only argument was the sword, and whose only paradise was a brothel. No Gothic scourge of God, no Vandal pest of nations, no fabled fugitive from the flames of Troy, no bastard Norman tyrant, appears among the list of worthies who first landed on the rock, which your veneration has preserved as a lasting monument of their achievement. The great actors of the day we now solemnize were illustrious by their intrepid valor no less than by their Christian graces, but the clarion of conquest has not blazoned forth their names to all the winds of heaven. Their glory has not been wafted over oceans of blood to the remotest regions of the earth. They have not erected to themselves colossal statues upon pedestals of human bones, to provoke and insult the tardy hand of heavenly retribution. But theirs was "the better fortitude of patience and heroic martyrdom." Theirs was the gentle temper of Christian kindness; the rigorous observance of reciprocal justice; the unconquerable soul of conscious integrity. Worldly fame has been parsimonious of her favor to the memory of those generous companions. Their numbers were small; their stations in life obscure; the object of their enterprise unostentatious; the theatre of their exploits remote; how could they possibly be favorites of worldly Fame—that common crier, whose existence is only known by the assemblage of multitudes; that pander of wealth and greatness, so eager to haunt the palaces of fortune, and so fastidious to the houseless dignity of virtue; that parasite of pride, ever scornful to meekness, and ever obsequious to insolent power; that heedless trumpeter, whose ears are deaf to modest merit, and whose eyes are blind to bloodless, distant excellence?

When the persecuted companions of Robinson, exiles from their native land, anxiously sued for the privilege of removing a thousand leagues more distant to an untried soil, a rigorous climate, and a savage wilderness, for the sake of reconciling their sense of religious duty with their affections for their country, few, perhaps none of them, formed a conception of what would be, within two centuries, the result of their undertaking. When the jealous and niggardly policy of their British sovereign denied them even that humblest of requests, and instead of liberty would barely consent to promise connivance, neither he nor they might be aware that they were laying the foundations of a power, and that he was sowing the seeds of a spirit, which, in less than two hundred years, would stagger the throne of his descendants, and shake his united kingdoms to the centre. So far is it from the ordinary habits of mankind to calculate the importance of events in their elementary principles, that had the first colonists of our country ever intimated as a part of their designs the project of founding a great and mighty nation, the finger of scorn would have pointed them to the cells of bedlam as an abode more suitable for hatching vain empires than the solitude of a transatlantic desert.

These consequences, then so little foreseen, have unfolded themselves, in all their grandeur, to the eyes of the present age. It is a common amusement of speculative minds to contrast the magnitude of the most important events with the minuteness of their primeval causes, and the records of mankind are full of examples for such contemplations. It is, however, a more profitable employment to trace the constituent principles of future greatness in their kernel; to detect in the acorn at our feet the germ of that majestic oak, whose roots shoot down to the centre, and whose branches aspire to the skies. Let it be, then, our present occupation to inquire and endeavor to ascertain the causes first put in operation at the period of our commemoration, and already productive of such magnificent effects; to examine with reiterated care and minute attention the characters of those men who gave the first impulse to a new series of events in the history of the world; to applaud and emulate those qualities of their minds which we shall find deserving of our admiration; to recognize with candor those features which forbid approbation or even require censure, and, finally, to lay alike their frailties and their perfections to our own hearts, either as warning or as example.

Of the various European settlements upon this continent, which have finally merged in one independent nation, the first establishments were made at various times, by several nations, and under the influence of different motives. In many instances, the conviction of religious obligation formed one and a powerful inducement of the adventures; but in none, excepting the settlement at Plymouth, did they constitute the sole and exclusive actuating cause. Worldly interest and commercial speculation entered largely into the views of other settlers, but the commands of conscience were the only stimulus to the emigrants from Leyden. Previous to their expedition hither, they had endured a long banishment from their native country. Under every species of discouragement, they undertook the vogage; they performed it in spite of numerous and almost insuperable obstacles; they arrived upon a wilderness bound with frost and hoary with snow, without the boundaries of their charter, outcasts from all human society, and coasted five weeks together, in the dead of winter, on this tempestuous shore, exposed at once to the fury of the elements, to the arrows of the native savage, and to the impending horrors of famine.

Courage and perseverance have a magical talisman, before which difficulties disappear and obstacles vanish into air. These qualities have ever been displayed in their mightiest perfection, as attendants in the retinue of strong passions. From the first discovery of the Western Hemisphere by Columbus until the settlement of Virginia which immediately preceded that of Plymouth, the various adventurers from the ancient world had exhibited upon innumerable occasions that ardor of enterprise and that stubbornness of pursuit which set all danger at defiance, and chained the violence of nature at their feet. But they were all instigated by personal interests. Avarice and ambition had tuned their souls to that pitch of exaltation. Selfish passions were the parents of their heroism. It was reserved for the first settlers of New England to perform achievements equally arduous, to trample down obstructions equally formidable, to dispel dangers equally terrific, under the single inspiration of conscience. To them even liberty herself was but a subordinate and secondary consideration. They claimed exemption from the mandates of human authority, as militating with their subjection to a superior power. Before the voice of heaven they silenced even the calls of their country.

Yet, while so deeply impressed with the sense of religious obligation, they felt, in all its energy, the force of that tender tie which binds the heart of every virtuous man to his native land. It was to renew that connection with their country which had been severed by their compulsory expatriation, that they resolved to face all the hazards of a perilous navigation and all the labors of a toilsome distant settlement. Under the mild protection of the Batavian government, they enjoyed already that freedom of religious worship, for which they had resigned so many comforts and enjoyments at home; but their hearts panted for a restoration to the bosom of their country. Invited and urged by the open-hearted and truly benevolent people who had given them an asylum from the persecution of their own kindred to form their settlement within the territories then under their jurisdiction, the love of their country predominated over every influence save that of conscience alone, and they preferred the precarious chance of relaxation from the bigoted rigor of the English government to the certain liberality and alluring offers of the Hollanders. Observe, my countrymen, the generous patriotism, the cordial union of soul, the conscious yet unaffected vigor which beam in their application to the British monarch:—

> "They were well weaned from the delicate milk of their mother country, and inured to the difficulties of a strange land. They were knit together in a strict and sacred bond, to take care of the good of each other and of the whole. It was not with them as with other men, whom small things could discourage, or small discontents cause to wish themselves again at home."

Children of these exalted Pilgrims! Is there one among you who can hear the simple and pathetic energy of these expressions without tenderness and admiration? Venerated shades of our forefathers! No, ye were, indeed, not ordinary men! That country which had ejected you so cruelly from her bosom you still delighted to contemplate in the character of an affectionate and beloved mother. The sacred bond which knit you together was indissoluble while you lived; and oh, may it be to your descendants the example and the pledge of harmony to the latest period of time! The difficulties and dangers, which so often had defeated attempts of similar establishments, were unable to subdue souls tempered like yours. You heard the rigid interdictions; you saw the menacing forms of toil and danger, forbidding your access to this land of promise; but you heard without dismay; you saw and disdained retreat. Firm and undaunted in the confidence of that sacred bond; conscious of the purity, and convinced of the importance of your motives, you put your trust in the protecting shield of Providence, and smiled defiance at the combining terrors of human malice and of elemental strife. These, in the accomplishment of your undertaking, you were summoned to encounter in their most hideous forms; these you met with that fortitude, and combatted with that perseverance, which you had promised in their anticipation; these you completely vanquished in establishing the foundations of New England, and the day which we now commemorate is the perpetual memorial of your triumph.

It were an occupation peculiarly pleasing to cull from our early historians, and exhibit before you every detail of this transaction; to carry you in imagination on board their bark at the first moment of her arrival in the bay; to accompany Carver, Winslow, Bradford, and Standish, in all their excursions upon the desolate coast; to follow them into every rivulet and creek where they endeavored to find a firm footing, and to fix, with a pause of delight and exultation, the instant when the first of these heroic adventurers alighted on the spot where you, their descendants, now enjoy the glorious and happy reward of their labors. But in this grateful task, your former orators, on this anniversary, have anticipated all that the most ardent industry could collect, and gratified all that the most inquisitive curiosity could desire. To you, my friends, every occurrence of that momentous period is already familiar. A transient allusion to a few characteristic instances, which mark the peculiar history of the

Plymouth settlers, may properly supply the place of a narrative, which, to this auditory, must be superfluous.

One of these remarkable incidents is the execution of that instrument of government by which they formed themselves into a body politic, the day after their arrival upon the coast, and previous to their first landing. This is, perhaps, the only instance in human history of that positive, original social compact, which speculative philosophers have imagined as the only legitimate source of government. Here was a unanimous and personal assent, by all the individuals of the community, to the association by which they became a nation. It was the result of circumstances and discussions which had occurred during their passage from Europe, and is a full demonstration that the nature of civil government, abstracted from the political institutions of their native country, had been an object of their serious meditation. The settlers of all the former European colonies had contented themselves with the powers conferred upon them by their respective charters, without looking beyond the seal of the royal parchment for the measure of their rights and the rule of their duties. The founders of Plymouth had been impelled by the peculiarities of their situation to examine the subject with deeper and more comprehensive research. After twelve years of banishment from the land of their first allegiance, during which they had been under an adoptive and temporary subjection to another sovereign, they must naturally have been led to reflect upon the relative rights and duties of allegiance and subjection. They had resided in a city, the seat of a university, where the polemical and political controversies of the time were pursued with uncommon fervor. In this period they had witnessed the deadly struggle between the two parties, into which the people of the United Provinces, after their separation from the crown of Spain, had divided themselves. The contest embraced within its compass not only theological doctrines, but political principles, and Maurice and Barnevelt were the temporal leaders of the same rival factions, of which Episcopius and Polyander were the ecclesiastical champions.

That the investigation of the fundamental principles of government was deeply implicated in these dissensions is evident from the immortal work of Grotius, upon the rights of war and peace, which undoubtedly originated from them. Grotius himself had been a most distinguished actor and sufferer in those important scenes of internal convulsion, and his work was first published very shortly after the departure of our forefathers from Leyden. It is well known that in the course of the contest Mr. Robinson more than once appeared, with credit to himself, as a public disputant against Episcopius; and from the manner in which the fact is related by Governor Bradford, it is apparent that the whole English Church at Leyden took a zealous interest in the religious part of the controversy. As strangers in the land, it is presumable that they wisely and honorably avoided entangling themselves in the political contentions involved with it. Yet the theoretic principles, as they were drawn into discussion, could not fail to arrest their attention, and must have assisted them to form accurate ideas concerning the origin and extent of authority among men, independent of positive institutions. The importance of these circumstances will not be duly weighed without taking into consideration the state of opinion then prevalent in England. The general principles of government were there little understood and less examined. The whole substance of human authority was centred in the simple doctrine of royal prerogative, the origin of which was always traced in theory to divine institution. Twenty years later, the subject was more industriously sifted, and for half a century became one of the principal topics of controversy between the ablest and most enlightened men in the nation. The instrument of voluntary association executed on board the Mayflower testifies that the parties to it had anticipated the improvement of their nation.

Another incident, from which we may derive occasion for important reflections, was the attempt of these original settlers to establish among them that community of goods and of labor, which fanciful politicians, from the days of Plato to those of Rousseau, have recommended as the fundamental law of a perfect republic. This theory results, it must be acknowledged, from principles of reasoning most flattering to the human character. If industry, frugality, and disinterested integrity were alike the virtues of all, there would, apparently, be more of the social spirit, in making all property a common stock, and giving to each individual a proportional title to the wealth of the whole. Such is the basis upon which Plato forbids, in his Republic, the division of property. Such is the system upon which Rousseau pronounces the first man who enclosed a field with a fence, and, said, «This is mine,» a traitor to the human species. A wiser and more useful philosophy, however, directs us to consider man according to the nature in which he was formed; subject to infirmities, which no wisdom can remedy; to weaknesses, which no institution can strengthen; to vices, which no legislation can correct. Hence, it becomes obvious that separate property is the natural and indisputable right of separate exertion; that community of goods without community of toil is oppressive and unjust; that it counteracts the laws of nature, which prescribe that he only who sows the seed shall reap the harvest; that it discourages all energy, by destroying its rewards; and makes the most virtuous and active members of society the slaves and drudges of the worst. Such was the issue of this experiment among our forefathers, and the same event demonstrated the error of the system in the elder settlement of Virginia. Let us cherish that spirit of harmony which prompted our forefathers to make the attempt, under circumstances more favorable to its success than, perhaps, ever occurred upon earth. Let us no less admire the candor with which they relinquished it, upon discovering its irremediable inefficacy. To found principles of government upon too advantageous an estimate of the human character is an error of inexperience, the source of which is so amiable that it is impossible to censure it with severity. We have seen the same mistake, committed in our own age, and upon a larger theatre. Happily for our ancestors, their situation allowed them to repair it before its effects had proved destructive. They had no pride of vain philosophy to support, no perfidious rage of faction to glut, by persevering in their mistakes until they should be extinguished in torrents of blood.

As the attempt to establish among themselves the community of goods was a seal of that sacred bond which knit them so closely together, so the conduct they observed towards the natives of the country displays their steadfast adherence to the rules of justice and their faithful attachment to those of benevolence and charity.

No European settlement ever formed upon this continent has been more distinguished for undeviating kindness and equity towards the savages. There are, indeed, moralists who have questioned the right of the Europeans to intrude upon the possessions of the aboriginals in any case, and under any limitations whatsoever. But have they maturely considered the whole subject? The Indian right of possession itself stands, with regard to the greatest part of the country, upon a questionable foundation. Their cultivated fields; their constructed habitations; a space of ample sufficiency for their subsistence, and whatever they had annexed to themselves by personal labor, was undoubtedly, by the laws of nature, theirs. But what is the right of a huntsman to the forest of a thousand miles over which he has accidentally ranged in quest of prey? Shall the liberal bounties of Providence to the race of man be monopolized by one of ten thousand for whom they were created? Shall the exuberant bosom of the common mother, amply adequate to the nourishment of millions, be claimed exclusively by a few hundreds of her offspring? Shall the lordly savage not only disdain the virtues and enjoyments of civilization himself, but shall he control the civilization of a world? Shall he forbid the wilderness to blossom like a rose? Shall he forbid the oaks of the forest to fall before the ax of industry, and to rise again, transformed into the habitations of ease and elegance? Shall he doom an immense region of the globe to perpetual desolation, and to hear the howlings of the tiger and the wolf silence forever the voice of human gladness? Shall the fields and the valleys, which a beneficent God has formed to teem with the life of innumerable multitudes, be condemned to everlasting barrenness? Shall the mighty rivers, poured out by the hand of nature, as channels of communication between numerous nations, roll their waters in sullen silence and eternal solitude to the deep? Have hundreds of commodious harbors, a thousand leagues of coast, and a boundless ocean, been spread in the front of this land, and shall every purpose of utility to which they could apply be prohibited by the tenant of the woods? No, generous philanthropists! Heaven has not been thus inconsistent in the works of its hands. Heaven has not thus placed at irreconcilable strife its moral laws with its physical creation. The Pilgrims of Plymouth obtained their right of possession to the territory on which they settled, by titles as fair and unequivocal as any human property can be held. By their voluntary association they recognized their allegiance to the government of Britain, and in process of time received whatever powers and authorities could be conferred upon them by a charter from their sovereign. The spot on which they fixed had belonged to an Indian tribe, totally extirpated by that devouring pestilence which had swept the country shortly before their arrival. The territory, thus free from all exclusive possession, they might have taken by the natural right of occupancy. Desirous, however, of giving ample satisfaction to every pretense of prior right, by formal and solemn conventions with the chiefs of the neighboring tribes, they acquired the further security of a purchase. At their hands the children of the desert had no cause of complaint. On the great day of retribution, what thousands, what millions of the American race will appear at the bar of judgment to arraign their European invading conquerors! Let us humbly hope that the fathers of the Plymouth Colony will then appear in the whiteness of innocence. Let us indulge in the belief that they will not only be free from all accusation of injustice to these unfortunate sons of nature, but that the testimonials of their acts of kindness and benevolence towards them will plead the cause of their virtues, as they are now authenticated by the record of history upon earth.

Religious discord has lost her sting; the cumbrous weapons of theological warfare are antiquated; the field of politics supplies the alchemists of our times with materials of more fatal explosion, and the butchers of mankind no longer travel to another world for instruments of cruelty and destruction. Our age is too enlightened to contend upon topics which concern only the interests of eternity; the men who hold in proper contempt all controversies about trifles, except such as inflame their own passions, have made it a commonplace censure against your ancestors, that their zeal was enkindled by subjects of trivial importance; and that however aggrieved by the intolerance of others, they were alike intolerant themselves. Against these objections, your candid judgment will not require an unqualified justification; but your respect and gratitude for the founders of the State may boldly claim an ample apology. The original grounds of their separation from the Church of England were not objects of a magnitude to dissolve the bonds of communion, much less those of charity, between Christian brethren of the same essential principles. Some of them, however, were not inconsiderable, and numerous inducements concurred to give them an extraordinary interest in their eyes. When that portentous system of abuses, the Papal dominion, was overturned, a great variety of religious sects arose in its stead in the several countries, which for many centuries before had been screwed beneath its subjection. The fabric of the reformation, first undertaken in England upon a contracted basis, by a capricious and sanguinary tyrant, had been successively overthrown and restored, renewed and altered, according to the varying humors and principles of four successive monarchs. To ascertain the precise point of division between the genuine institutions of Christianity and the corruptions accumulated upon them in the progress of fifteen centuries, was found a task of extreme difficulty throughout the Christian world.

Men of the profoundest learning, of the sublimest genius, and of the purest integrity, after devoting their lives to the research, finally differed in their ideas upon many great points, both of doctrine and discipline. The main question, it was admitted on all hands, most intimately concerned the highest interests of man, both temporal and eternal. Can we wonder that men who felt their happiness here and their hopes of hereafter, their worldly welfare and the kingdom of heaven at stake, should sometimes attach an importance beyond their intrinsic weight to collateral points of controversy, connected with the all-involving object of the reformation? The changes in the forms and principles of religious worship were introduced and regulated in England by the hand of public authority. But that hand had not been uniform or steady in its operations. During the persecutions inflicted in the interval of Popish restoration under the reign of Mary, upon all who favored the reformation, many of the most zealous reformers had been compelled to fly their country. While residing on the continent of Europe, they had adopted the principles of the most complete and rigorous reformation, as taught and established by Calvin. On returning afterwards to their native country, they were dissatisfied with the partial reformation, at which, as they conceived, the English establishment had rested; and claiming the privilege of private conscience, upon which alone any departure from the Church of Rome could be justified, they insisted upon the right of adhering to the system of their own preference, and, of course, upon that of nonconformity to the establishment prescribed by the royal authority. The only means used to convince them of error and reclaim them from dissent was force, and force served but to confirm the opposition it was meant to suppress. By driving the founders of the Plymouth Colony into exile, it constrained them to absolute separation from the Church of England; and by the refusal afterwards to allow them a positive toleration, even in this American wilderness, the council of James I. rendered that separation irreconcilable. Viewing their religious liberties here, as held only by sufferance, yet bound to them by all the ties of conviction, and by all their sufferings for them, could they forbear to look upon every dissenter among themselves with a jealous eye? Within two years after their landing, they beheld a rival settlement attempted in their immediate neighborhood; and not long after, the laws of self-preservation compelled them to break up a nest of revelers, who boasted of protection from the mother country, and who had recurred to the easy but pernicious resource of feeding their wanton idleness, by furnishing the savages with the means, the skill, and the instruments of European destruction. Toleration, in that instance, would have been self-murder, and many other examples might be alleged, in which their necessary measures of self-defense have been exaggerated into cruelty, and their most indispensable precautions distorted into persecution. Yet shall we not pretend that they were exempt from the common laws of mortality, or entirely free from all the errors of their age. Their zeal might sometimes be too ardent, but it was always sincere. At this day, religious indulgence is one of our clearest duties, because it is one of our undisputed rights. While we rejoice that the principles of genuine Christianity have so far triumphed over the prejudices of a former generation, let us fervently hope for the day when it will prove equally victorious over the malignant passions of our own.

In thus calling your attention to some of the peculiar features in the principles, the character, and the history of our forefathers, it is as wide from my design, as I know it would be from your approbation, to adorn their memory with a chaplet plucked from the domain of others. The occasion and the day are more peculiarly devoted to them, and let it never be dishonored with a contracted and exclusive spirit. Our affections as citizens embrace the whole extent of the Union, and the names of Raleigh, Smith, Winthrop, Calvert, Penn, and Oglethorpe, excite in our minds recollections equally pleasing and gratitude equally fervent with those of Carver and Bradford. Two centuries have not yet elapsed since the first European foot touched the soil which now constitutes the American Union. Two centuries more and our numbers must exceed those of Europe itself. The destinies of this empire, as they appear in prospect before us, disdain the powers of human calculation. Yet, as the original founder of the Roman state is said once to have lifted upon his shoulders the fame and fortunes of all his posterity, so let us never forget that the glory and greatness of all our descendants is in our hands. Preserve in all their purity, refine, if possible, from all their alloy, those virtues which we this day commemorate as the ornament of our forefathers. Adhere to them with inflexible resolution, as to the horns of the altar; instill them with unwearied perseverance into the minds of your children; bind your souls and theirs to the national Union as the chords of life are centred in the heart, and you shall soar with rapid and steady wing to the summit of human glory. Nearly a century ago, one of those rare minds to whom it is given to discern future greatness in its seminal principles upon contemplating the situation of this continent, pronounced, in a vein of poetic inspiration, « Westward the star of empire takes its way.» Let us unite in ardent supplication to the Founder of nations and the Builder of worlds, that what then was prophecy may continue unfolding into history,—that the dearest hopes of the human race may not be extinguished in disappointment, and that the last may prove the noblest empire of time.

LAFAYETTE

(Delivered in Congress, December 31st, 1834)

On the sixth of September, 1757, Lafayette was born. The kings of France and Britain were seated upon their thrones by virtue of the principle of hereditary succession, variously modified and blended with different forms of religious faith, and they were waging war against each other, and exhausting the blood and treasure of their people for causes in which neither of the nations had any beneficial or lawful interest.

In this war the father of Lafayette fell in the cause of his king but not of his country. He was an officer of an invading army, the instrument of his sovereign's wanton ambition and lust of conquest. The people of the electorate of Hanover had done no wrong to him or to his country. When his son came to an age capable of understanding the irreparable loss that he had suffered, and to reflect upon the causes of his father's fate, there was no drop of consolation mingled in the cup from the consideration that he had died for his country. And when the youthful mind was awakened to meditation upon the rights of mankind, the principles of freedom, and theories of government, it cannot be difficult to perceive in the illustrations of his own family records the source of that aversion to hereditary rule, perhaps the most distinguishing feature of his own political opinions, and to which he adhered through all the vicissitudes of his life. . . .

Lafayette was born a subject of the most absolute and most splendid monarchy of Europe, and in the highest rank of her proud and chivalrous nobility. He had been educated at a college of the University of Paris, founded by the royal munificence of Louis XIV., or Cardinal Richelieu. Left an orphan in early childhood, with the inheritance of a princely fortune, he had been married, at sixteen years of age, to a daughter of the house of Noailles, the most distinguished family of the kingdom, scarcely deemed in public consideration inferior to that which wore the crown. He came into active life, at the change from boy to man, a husband and a father, in the full enjoyment of everything that avarice could covet, with a certain prospect before him of all that ambition could crave. Happy in his domestic affections, incapable, from the benignity of his nature, of envy, hatred, or revenge, a life of «ignoble ease and indolent repose» seemed to be that which nature and fortune had combined to prepare before him. To men of ordinary mold this condition would have led to a life of luxurious apathy and sensual indulgence. Such was the life into which, from the operation of the same causes, Louis XV. had sunk, with his household and court, while Lafayette was rising to manhood surrounded by the contamination of their example. Had his natural endowments been even of the higher and nobler order of such as adhere to virtue, even in the lap of prosperity, and in the bosom of temptation, he might have lived and died a pattern of the nobility of France, to be classed, in aftertimes, with the Turennes and the Montausiers of the age of Louis XIV., or with the Villars or the Lamoignons of the age immediately preceding his own.

But as, in the firmament of heaven that rolls over our heads, there is, among the stars of the first magnitude, one so pre-eminent in splendor as, in the opinion of astronomers, to constitute a class by itself, so in the fourteen hundred years of the French monarchy, among the multitudes of great and mighty men which it has evolved, the name of Lafayette stands unrivaled in the solitude of glory.

In entering upon the threshold of life, a career was to open before him. He had the option of the court and the camp. An office was tendered to him in the household of the King's brother, the Count de Provence, since successively a royal exile and a reinstated king. The servitude and inaction of a court had no charms for him; he preferred a commission in the army, and, at the time of the Declaration of Independence, was a captain of dragoons in garrison at Metz.

There, at an entertainment given by his relative, the Marechal de Broglie, the commandant of the place, to the Duke of Gloucester, brother to the British king, and then a transient traveler through that part of France, he learns, as an incident of intelligence received that morning by the English Prince from London, that the congress of rebels at Philadelphia had issued a Declaration of Independence. A conversation ensues upon the causes which have contributed to produce this event, and upon the consequences which may be expected to flow from it. The imagination of Lafayette has caught across the Atlantic tide the spark emitted from the Declaration of Independence; his heart has kindled at the shock, and, before he slumbers upon his pillow, he has resolved to devote his life and fortune to the cause.

You have before you the cause and the man. The self-devotion of Lafayette was twofold. First to the people, maintaining a bold and seemingly desperate struggle against oppression, and for national existence. Secondly, and chiefly, to the principles of their declaration, which then first unfurled before his eyes the consecrated standard of human rights. To that standard, without an instant of hesitation, he repaired. Where it would lead him, it is scarcely probable that he himself then foresaw. It was then identical with the Stars and Stripes of the American Union, floating to the breeze from the Hall of Independence, at Philadelphia. Nor sordid avarice, nor vulgar ambition, could point his footsteps to the pathway leading to that banner. To the love of ease or pleasure nothing could be more repulsive. Something may be allowed to the beatings of the youthful breast, which make ambition virtue, and something to the spirit of military adventure, imbibed from his profession, and which he felt in common with many others. France, Germany, Poland, furnished to the armies of this Union, in our revolutionary struggle, no inconsiderable number of officers of high rank and distinguished merit. The names of Pulaski and De Kalb are numbered among the martyrs of our freedom, and their ashes repose in our soil side by side with the canonized bones of Warren and of Montgomery. To the virtues of Lafayette, a more protracted career and happier earthly destinies were reserved. To the moral principle of political action, the sacrifices of no other man were comparable to his. Youth, health, fortune; the favor of his king; the enjoyment of ease and pleasure; even the choicest blessings of domestic felicity—he gave them all for toil and danger in a distant land, and an almost hopeless cause; but it was the cause of justice, and of the rights of human kind. . . .

Pronounce him one of the first men of his age, and you have not yet done him justice. Try him by that test to which he sought in vain to stimulate the vulgar and selfish spirit of Napoleon; class him among the men who, to compare and seat themselves, must take in the compass of all ages; turn back your eyes upon the records of time, summon from the creation of the world to this day the mighty dead of every age and every clime—and where, among the race of merely mortal men, shall one be found, who, as the benefactor of his kind, shall claim to take precedence of Lafayette?

There have doubtless been, in all ages, men whose discoveries or inventions, in the world of matter or of mind, have opened new avenues to the dominion of man over the material creation; have increased his means or his faculties of enjoyment; have raised him in nearer approximation to that higher and happier condition, the object of his hopes and aspirations in his present state of existence.

Lafayette discovered no new principle of politics or of morals. He invented nothing in science. He disclosed no new phenomenon in the laws of nature. Born and educated in the highest order of feudal nobility, under the most absolute monarchy of Europe, in possession of an affluent fortune, and master of himself and of all his capabilities, at the moment of attaining manhood the principle of republican justice and of social equality took possession of his heart and mind, as if by inspiration from above. He devoted himself, his life, his fortune, his hereditary honors, his towering ambition, his splendid hopes, all to the cause of liberty. He came to another hemisphere to defend her. He became one of the most effective champions of our independence; but, that once achieved, he returned to his own country, and thenceforward took no part in the controversies which have divided us. In the events of our revolution, and in the forms of policy which we have adopted for the establishment and perpetuation of our freedom, Lafayette found the most perfect form of government. He wished to add nothing to it. He would gladly have abstracted nothing from it. Instead of the imaginary republic of Plato, or the Utopia of Sir Thomas Moore, he took a practical existing model, in actual operation here, and never attempted or wished more than to apply it faithfully to his own country.

It was not given to Moses to enter the promised land; but he saw it from the summit of Pisgah. It was not given to Lafayette to witness the consummation of his wishes in the establishment of a republic and the extinction of all hereditary rule in France. His principles were in advance of the age and hemisphere in which he lived. A Bourbon still reigns on the throne of France, and it is not for us to scrutinize the title by which he reigns. The principles of elective and hereditary power, blended in reluctant union in his person, like the red and white roses of York and Lancaster, may postpone to aftertime the last conflict to which they must ultimately come. The life of the patriarch was not long enough for the development of his whole political system. Its final accomplishment is in the womb of time.

The anticipation of this event is the more certain, from the consideration that all the principles for which Lafayette contended were practical. He never indulged himself in wild and fanciful speculations. The principle of hereditary power was, in his opinion, the bane of all republican liberty in Europe. Unable to extinguish it in the Revolution of 1830, so far as concerned the chief magistracy of the nation, Lafayette had the satisfaction of seeing it abolished with reference to the peerage. An hereditary crown, stript of the support which it may derive from an hereditary peerage, however compatible with Asiatic despotism, is an anomaly in the history of the Christian world, and in the theory of free government. There is no argument producible against the existence of an hereditary peerage but applies with aggravated weight against the transmission, from sire to son, of an hereditary crown. The prejudices and passions of the people of France rejected the principle of inherited power, in every station of public trust, excepting the first and highest of them all;

but there they clung to it, as did the Israelites of old to the savory deities of Egypt.

This is not the time nor the place for a disquisition upon the comparative merits, as a system of government, of a republic, and a monarchy surrounded by republican institutions. Upon this subject there is among us no diversity of opinion; and if it should take the people of France another half century of internal and external war, of dazzling and delusive glories; of unparalleled triumphs, humiliating reverses, and bitter disappointments, to settle it to their satisfaction, the ultimate result can only bring them to the point where we have stood from the day of the Declaration of Independence — to the point where Lafayette would have brought them, and to which he looked as a consummation devoutly to be wished.

Then, too, and then only, will be the time when the character of Lafayette will be appreciated at its true value throughout the civilized world. When the principle of hereditary dominion shall be extinguished in all the institutions of France; when government shall no longer be considered as property transmissible from sire to son, but as a trust committed for a limited time, and then to return to the people whence it came; as a burdensome duty to be discharged, and not as a reward to be abused; when a claim, any claim, to political power by inheritance shall, in the estimation of the whole French people, be held as it now is by the whole people of the North American Union — then will be the time for contemplating the character of Lafayette, not merely in the events of his life, but in the full development of his intellectual conceptions, of his fervent aspirations, of the labors and perils and sacrifices of his long and eventful career upon earth; and thenceforward, till the hour when the trump of the Archangel shall sound to announce that Time shall be no more, the name of Lafayette shall stand enrolled upon the annals of our race, high on the list of the pure and disinterested benefactors of mankind.

THE JUBILEE OF THE CONSTITUTION

(Delivered at New York, April 30th, 1839)

Fellow-Citizens and Brethren, Associates of the New York Historical Society:—

WOULD it be an unlicensed trespass of the imagination to conceive that on the night preceding the day of which you now commemorate the fiftieth anniversary—on the night preceding that thirtieth of April, 1789, when from the balcony of your city hall the chancellor of the State of New York administered to George Washington the solemn oath faithfully to execute the office of President of the United States, and to the best of his ability to preserve, protect, and defend the Constitution of the United States—that in the visions of the night the guardian angel of the Father of our country had appeared before him, in the venerated form of his mother, and, to cheer and encourage him in the performance of the momentous and solemn duties that he was about to assume, had delivered to him a suit of celestial armor—a helmet, consisting of the principles of piety, of justice, of honor, of benevolence, with which from his earliest infancy he had hitherto walked through life, in the presence of all his brethren; a spear, studded with the self-evident truths of the Declaration of Independence; a sword, the same with which he had led the armies of his country through the war of freedom to the summit of the triumphal arch of independence; a corslet and cuishes of long experience and habitual intercourse in peace and war with the world of mankind, his contemporaries of the human race, in all their stages of civilization; and, last of all, the Constitution of the United States, a shield, embossed by heavenly hands with the future history of his country.

Yes, gentlemen, on that shield the Constitution of the United States was sculptured (by forms unseen, and in characters then invisible to mortal eye), the predestined and prophetic history of the one confederated people of the North American Union.

They had been the settlers of thirteen separate and distinct English colonies, along the margin of the shore of the North American continent; contiguously situated, but chartered by adventurers of characters variously diversified, including sectarians, religious and political, of all the classes which for the two preceding centuries had agitated and divided the people of the

British islands—and with them were intermingled the descendants of Hollanders, Swedes, Germans, and French fugitives from the persecution of the revoker of the Edict of Nantes.

In the bosoms of this people, thus heterogeneously composed, there was burning, kindled at different furnaces, but all furnaces of affliction, one clear, steady flame of liberty. Bold and daring enterprise, stubborn endurance of privation, unflinching intrepidity in facing danger, and inflexible adherence to conscientious principle, had steeled to energetic and unyielding hardihood the characters of the primitive settlers of all these colonies. Since that time two or three generations of men had passed away, but they had increased and multiplied with unexampled rapidity; and the land itself had been the recent theatre of a ferocious and bloody seven-years' war between the two most powerful and most civilized nations of Europe contending for the possession of this continent.

Of that strife the victorious combatant had been Britain. She had conquered the provinces of France. She had expelled her rival totally from the continent, over which, bounding herself by the Mississippi, she was thenceforth to hold divided empire only with Spain. She had acquired undisputed control over the Indian tribes still tenanting the forests unexplored by the European man. She had established an uncontested monopoly of the commerce of all her colonies. But forgetting all the warnings of preceding ages—forgetting the lessons written in the blood of her own children, through centuries of departed time, she undertook to tax the people of the colonies without their consent.

Resistance, instantaneous, unconcerted, sympathetic, inflexible resistance, like an electric shock, startled and roused the people of all the English colonies on this continent.

This was the first signal of the North American Union. The struggle was for chartered rights—for English liberties—for the cause of Algernon Sidney and John Hampden—for trial by jury—the Habeas Corpus and Magna Charta.

But the English lawyers had decided that Parliament was omnipotent—and Parliament, in its omnipotence, instead of trial by jury and the Habeas Corpus, enacted admiralty courts in England to try Americans for offenses charged against them as committed in America; instead of the privileges of Magna Charta, nullified the charter itself of Massachusetts Bay; shut up the port of Boston; sent armies and navies to keep the peace and teach the colonies that John Hampden was a rebel and Algernon Sidney a traitor.

English liberties had failed them. From the omnipotence of Parliament the Colonists appealed to the rights of man and the omnipotence of the God of battles. Union! Union! was the instinctive and simultaneous cry throughout the land. Their congress, assembled at Philadelphia, once — twice — had petitioned the king; had remonstrated to Parliament; had addressed the people of Britain, for the rights of Englishmen — in vain. Fleets and armies, the blood of Lexington, and the fires of Charlestown and Falmouth, had been the answer to petition, remonstrance, and address. . . .

The dissolution of allegiance to the British crown, the severance of the colonies from the British empire, and their actual existence as independent States, were definitively established in fact, by war and peace. The independence of each separate State had never been declared of right. It never existed in fact. Upon the principles of the Declaration of Independence, the dissolution of the ties of allegiance, the assumption of sovereign power, and the institution of civil government, are all acts of transcendent authority, which the people alone are competent to perform; and, accordingly, it is in the name and by the authority of the people, that two of these acts — the dissolution of allegiance, with the severance from the British empire, and the declaration of the United Colonies, as free and independent States, were performed by that instrument.

But there still remained the last and crowning act, which the people of the Union alone were competent to perform — the institution of civil government, for that compound nation, the United States of America.

At this day it cannot but strike us as extraordinary, that it does not appear to have occurred to any one member of that assembly, which had laid down in terms so clear, so explicit, so unequivocal, the foundation of all just government, in the imprescriptible rights of man, and the transcendent sovereignty of the people, and who in those principles had set forth their only personal vindication from the charges of rebellion against their king, and of treason to their country, that their last crowning act was still to be performed upon the same principles. That is, the institution, by the people of the United States, of a civil government, to guard and protect and defend them all. On the contrary, that same assembly which issued the Declaration of Independence, instead of continuing to act in the name and by the authority of the good people of the United States, had, immediately after the appointment of the committee to prepare the Declaration, appointed another committee, of one member from each colony, to prepare and digest the form of confederation to be entered into between the colonies.

That committee reported on the twelfth of July, eight days after the Declaration of Independence had been issued, a draft of articles of confederation between the colonies. This draft was prepared by John Dickinson, then a delegate from Pennsylvania, who voted against the Declaration of Independence, and never signed it, having been superseded by a new election of delegates from that State, eight days after his draft was reported.

There was thus no congeniality of principle between the Declaration of Independence and the articles of confederation. The foundation of the former was a superintending Providence—the rights of man, and the constituent revolutionary power of the people. That of the latter was the sovereignty of organized power, and the independence of the separate or dis-united States. The fabric of the Declaration and that of the confederation were each consistent with its own foundation, but they could not form one consistent, symmetrical edifice. They were the productions of different minds and of adverse passions; one, ascending for the foundation of human government to the laws of nature and of God, written upon the heart of man; the other, resting upon the basis of human institutions, and prescriptive law, and colonial charter. The corner stone of the one was right, that of the other was power. . . .

Where, then, did each State get the sovereignty, freedom, and independence, which the articles of confederation declare it retains?—not from the whole people of the whole Union—not from the Declaration of Independence—not from the people of the State itself. It was assumed by agreement between the legislatures of the several States, and their delegates in Congress, without authority from or consultation of the people at all.

In the Declaration of Independence, the enacting and constituent party dispensing and delegating sovereign power is the whole people of the United Colonies. The recipient party, invested with power, is the United Colonies, declared United States.

In the articles of confederation, this order of agency is inverted. Each State is the constituent and enacting party, and the United States in Congress assembled the recipient of delegated power—and that power delegated with such a penurious and carking hand that it had more the aspect of a revocation of the Declaration of Independence than an instrument to carry it into effect.

None of these indispensably necessary powers were ever conferred by the State legislatures upon the Congress of the federation; and well was it that they never were. The system itself was radically defective. Its incurable disease was an apostasy from the principles of the Declaration of Independence. A substitution of separate State sovereignties, in the place of the constituent sovereignty of the people, was the basis of the Confederate Union.

In the Congress of the confederation, the master minds of James Madison and Alexander Hamilton were constantly engaged through the closing years of the Revolutionary War and those of peace which immediately succeeded. That of John Jay was associated with them shortly after the peace, in the capacity of secretary to the Congress for foreign affairs. The incompetency of the articles of confederation for the management of the affairs of the Union at home and abroad was demonstrated to them by the painful and mortifying experience of every day. Washington, though in retirement, was brooding over the cruel injustice suffered by his associates in arms, the warriors of the Revolution; over the prostration of the public credit and the faith of the nation, in the neglect to provide for the payment even of the interest upon the public debt; over the disappointed hopes of the friends of freedom; in the language of the address from Congress to the States of the eighteenth of April, 1783—«the pride and boast of America, that the rights for which she contended were the rights of human nature.»

At his residence at Mount Vernon, in March 1785, the first idea was started of a revisal of the articles of confederation, by an organization, of means differing from that of a compact between the State legislatures and their own delegates in Congress. A convention of delegates from the State legislatures, independent of the Congress itself, was the expedient which presented itself for effecting the purpose, and an augmentation of the powers of Congress for the regulation of commerce, as the object for which this assembly was to be convened. In January 1786 the proposal was made and adopted in the legislature of Virginia, and communicated to the other State legislatures.

The convention was held at Annapolis, in September of that year. It was attended by delegates from only five of the central States, who, on comparing their restricted powers with the glaring and universally acknowledged defects of the confederation, reported only a recommendation for the assemblage of another convention of delegates to meet at Philadelphia, in May 1787, from all the States, and with enlarged powers.

The Constitution of the United States was the work of this convention. But in its construction the convention immediately perceived that they must retrace their steps, and fall back from a league of friendship between sovereign States to the constituent sovereignty of the people; from power to right—from the irresponsible despotism of State sovereignty to the self-evident truths of the Declaration of Independence. In that instrument, the right to institute and to alter governments among men was ascribed exclusively to the people—the ends of government were declared to be to secure the natural rights of man; and that when the government degenerates from the promotion to the destruction of that end, the right and the duty accrues to the people to dissolve this degenerate government and to institute another. The signers of the Declaration further averred, that the one people of the United Colonies were then precisely in that situation—with a government degenerated into tyranny, and called upon by the laws of nature and of nature's God to dissolve that government and to institute another. Then, in the name and by the authority of the good people of the colonies, they pronounced the dissolution of their allegiance to the king, and their eternal separation from the nation of Great Britain—and declared the United Colonies independent States. And here as the representatives of the one people they had stopped. They did not require the confirmation of this act, for the power to make the declaration had already been conferred upon them by the people, delegating the power, indeed, separately in the separate colonies, not by colonial authority, but by the spontaneous revolutionary movement of the people in them all.

From the day of that Declaration, the constituent power of the people had never been called into action. A confederacy had been substituted in the place of a government, and State sovereignty had usurped the constituent sovereignty of the people.

The convention assembled at Philadelphia had themselves no direct authority from the people. Their authority was all derived from the State legislatures. But they had the articles of confederation before them, and they saw and felt the wretched condition into which they had brought the whole people, and that the Union itself was in the agonies of death. They soon perceived that the indispensably needed powers were such as no State government, no combination of them, was by the principles of the Declaration of Independence competent to bestow. They could emanate only from the people. A highly respectable portion of the assembly, still clinging to the confederacy of States, proposed, as a substitute for the Constitution, a mere revival of the articles of confederation, with a grant of additional powers to the Congress. Their plan was respectfully and thoroughly discussed, but the want of a government and of the sanction of the people to the delegation of powers happily prevailed. A constitution for the people, and the distribution of legislative, executive, and judicial powers was prepared. It announced itself as the work of the people themselves; and as this was unquestionably a power assumed by the convention, not delegated to them by the people, they religiously confined it to a simple power to propose, and carefully provided that it should be no more than a proposal until sanctioned by the confederation Congress, by the State legislatures, and by the people of the several States, in conventions specially assembled, by authority of their legislatures, for the single purpose of examining and passing upon it.

And thus was consummated the work commenced by the Declaration of Independence — a work in which the people of the North American Union, acting under the deepest sense of responsibility to the Supreme Ruler of the universe, had achieved the most transcendent act of power that social man in his mortal condition can perform — even that of dissolving the ties of allegiance by which he is bound to his country; of renouncing that country itself; of demolishing its government; of instituting another government; and of making for himself another country in its stead.

And on that day, of which you now commemorate the fiftieth anniversary,— on that thirtieth day of April, 1789,— was this mighty revolution, not only in the affairs of our own country, but in the principles of government over civilized man, accomplished.

The revolution itself was a work of thirteen years—and had never been completed until that day. The Declaration of Independence and the Constitution of the United States are parts of one consistent whole, founded upon one and the same theory of government, then new in practice, though not as a theory, for it had been working itself into the mind of man for many ages, and had been especially expounded in the writings of Locke, though it had never before been adopted by a great nation in practice.

There are yet, even at this day, many speculative objections to this theory. Even in our own country, there are still philosophers who deny the principles asserted in the Declaration, as self-evident truths—who deny the natural equality and inalienable rights of man—who deny that the people are the only legitimate source of power—who deny that all just powers of government are derived from the consent of the governed. Neither your time, nor perphaps the cheerful nature of this occasion, permit me here to enter upon the examination of this anti-revolutionary theory, which arrays State sovereignty against the constituent sovereignty of the people, and distorts the Constitution of the United States into a league of friendship between confederate corporations. I speak to matters of fact. There is the Declaration of Independence, and there is the Constitution of the United States—let them speak for themselves. The grossly immoral and dishonest doctrine of despotic State sovereignty, the exclusive judge of its own obligations, and responsible to no power on earth or in heaven, for the violation of them, is not there. The Declaration says, it is not in me. The Constitution says, it is not in me.

www.ingramcontent.com/pod-product-compliance
Lightning Source LLC
La Vergne TN
LVHW091941060326
832903LV00043B/13

* 9 7 8 1 1 6 1 5 6 8 1 5 8 *